TESTIMONIAL

T0289443

"Eugene Gold is a master mentor! His insight on these changing times is a guide to the evolution of business and success. This book is a must read for anyone looking to move to the next level!"

-Dame Shellie A.Hunt
    Founder and CEO of the *Women of Global Change*

"As entrepreneurs, we must always give our best. But it's not just about working hard, it's about working smart. Eugene's book carries weight in the entrepreneurial community because of the smart approach he shares for building great companies. Every person looking to take charge of his/her personal and professional life should study Eugene's philosophies."

-Scott Duffy
    TV/online personality, keynote speaker and business coach

"Eugene Gold draws on the wisdom of some of the greatest thinkers in history and gives them a modern context. In these crazy unchartered waters we are now in, this book is a must read for anyone willing to welcome incredible new opportunities as well as face a new set of challenges."

-Larry Namer
    Co-Founder of *E! Entertainment Network* and media entrepreneur

FINDING THE AMERICAN DREAM

EUGENE GOLD

ISBN 978-1-7345585-6-2 (pbk)
ISBN 978-1-7345585-7-9 (hardcover)
ISBN 978-1-7345585-5-5 (e-book)

SHARE YOUR KNOWLEDGE.
IT IS A WAY TO
ACHIEVE IMMORTALITY.

DALAI LAMA XIV

CONTENTS

INTRODUCTION
WHY YOU NEED THIS BOOK

Does it feel sometimes as if you are stuck, with no way out? That you are doing everything that you need to, and yet your career is just not moving forward? You push hard, you give it your all, and you try your best — and still nothing happens?

It was like that for me, as well. But because I was able to break the chains and set myself free, I was able to achieve tremendous business growth in a very short time. And so I want to share the nontraditional philosophies, techniques, and tools that ultimately had an impact on my personal and professional life.

Initially, I began writing this book for my kids. My colleagues suggested I publish my success story for everyone to read. What you will uncover inside has already helped hundreds of people to achieve their career goals, to get where they want to be. While our goals may differ, and our successes may be defined in different ways, I am certain you will find very valuable advice in this book to help you to fulfill your dreams.

I wrote this book and kept it short on purpose. There is no fluff, no BS, no beating around the bush, no taking it easy.

I will show you that you actually possess almost everything you need to achieve anything that you desire.

I know, because I did it with no investments, no handouts, no rich parents, and no political hookups — just the strategies and techniques you will read here.

Read on. You have nothing to lose and simply everything to gain. Your current enrollment in whatever online course of some version of "Become a Super Rich, Mega Millionaire through [insert gimmick here]" can wait a day, right?

Now, let's get started!

SECTION 1.

TRADITIONAL PATH IS CROWDED

CHAPTER 1

FINDING THE AMERICAN DREAM

I believe that 'the traditional American dream' is dead.

Look, I realize that is a very bold statement to make. But please bear with me for a moment and let me explain a bit.

The thing is, I think the American Dream that my parents and society believed in for many years simply does not exist the way it used to.

So what do I mean by the American Dream? Pretty much what everyone has been telling about for decades and decades, which goes something like this:

> "Be a good boy or girl.
> "Go to school; then go to college and graduate.
> "You're going to get a very good job.
> "You will find the love of your life, and you're going to get a nice house with a white little fence around it and a nice, affordable mortgage.
> "You're going to have three kids and about seven grandkids, retire, and, finally, die happily."

ONE DAY A YOUNG STUDENT ASKED HIS PROFESSOR, "WHAT'S THE DIFFERENCE BETWEEN SCHOOL AND LIFE?"

THE PROFESSOR REPLIED, "IN SCHOOL, YOU´RE TAUGHT A LESSON AND THEN YOU´RE GIVEN A TEST. IN LIFE, YOU´RE GIVEN A TEST THAT TEACHES YOU A LESSON."

Now, I believe that the American Dream as I have described it above definitely existed as a reality in the past — roughly about forty years ago — in which you could get a degree and you could pretty much attend almost any university without financial difficulties. After you got your college degree, you were pretty much guaranteed to get a good paying job. The cost of education was not nearly as cost prohibitive, housing costs were nowhere near as high as now, and everything else was manageably affordable.

Nowadays, that American dream is not possible, because most of us live paycheck to paycheck. At least 50 percent of our salary covers the rent or mortgage, and the remainder goes for food and other necessities, with almost nothing left for savings. Why? All the loans you took using your credit cards: for furniture, vacations, little Suzie's braces. The cost of healthcare has gone sky high and payment on student debt the rest of your income.

Although all this may sound familiar to you, I also believe the American Dream has evolved. Just as technology and everything is improving, the same thing with the American Dream. So, if you actually want to achieve the American Dream, there must be new ways to accomplish it. I was lucky enough to find one such successful way.

So, a little bit about me: I came to the United States when I was 14, and I was a very good student in school. I graduated high school in three years instead of four. After that, I knew that in order to get a good-paying job I needed to get a bachelor's degree.

I worked two full-time jobs while I went to full-time college for my bachelor's in Business Management, and I had that bachelor's degree in under two years. (Payments on my student debt then started to kick in, yet I still didn't have a career to speak of.)

My peers explained to me that a bachelor's degree means nothing in today's economy, and, for me to be competitive and move forward, I actually needed a master's degree. *Sounds good! Let's go for a master's!*

And so I went for an MBA in finance, thinking that would give me the biggest advantage, and my road to a $100,000 a year salary would be assured. After I got my MBA in six months, with perfect grades and everything, I still couldn't get a job. Furthermore, after investing so much time and money in myself, I couldn't even get a promotion in my current job.

Where was this promised dream, the American Dream? I was painfully aware that I had read hundreds of resumés, interviews, and career

GAMES ARE WON BY PLAYERS WHO FOCUS ON THE PLAYING FIELD - NOT BY THOSE WHOSE EYES ARE GLUED TO THE SCOREBOARD.

-WARREN BUFFET

development books. I had spent scores of hours sending literally thousands of resumés to employers and headhunters. I had applied for hundreds of jobs, still, no job for me.

After many months of job hunting, sending resumes, attending interviews I was finally able to secure a banker position for a major bank. Compared to working two jobs for $9 per hour, hitting $16 per hour was a break I desperately needed. Nevertheless, I still didn't see a difference in my budget.

Was I that bad in handling my own finances? How can I be called a banker when I couldn't even help myself financially? The answer was right in front of me: more money earned, more taxes paid. And when all my student loans kicked in for my bachelor and master degrees, there was almost no difference from where I was now, financially, compared to before I got my masters.

So what *did* change? Well, having finished my schooling, I had more time to polish my skills, and my job came with commissioned earnings.

Thus, the more products I sold, the more I earned.

To make more money, I needed to learn how to push products much more efficiently. I needed to showcase my skills and proudly demonstrate to the company that I am a big producer and a

valuable asset to them.
After earning a lot of money for the company and their shareholders, they surely will recognize my talents and promote me further, or so I thought. My genius career plan was established.

I spent the next six months improving my skills, investing all the time I had towards increasing my value to the company. I became the top banker in my branch in the district, and then I moved quickly towards becoming a top banking employee nationwide. When the opportunity finally presented itself and a plum position was available — I lost it to the boss's nephew.

I gave this company my all and did everything right. I was earning the company 4 or 5 times what I was being paid. I was punctual, worked long hours, and I was outperforming my colleagues. I was proud of what I had done, and I even got a personal note of praise from the company's president. Clients would wait in line to see me, send me gifts for my customer service, and my higher-ups were singing my praises. So, when I put myself up for that promotion and lost it based on nepotism, I was angry beyond belief. I felt used and betrayed — even worse, I felt that I was replaceable.

Enough! I decided right then that I will never, EVER again allow someone else to decide what my American Dream should be!!!

A **SHARK** IN A FISH **TANK WILL** GROW 8 INCHES, BUT IN THE OCEAN **IT WILL** GROW TO 8 FEET OR MORE. THE **SHARK WILL** NEVER **OUTGROW ITS** ENVIROMENT AND THE SAME IS TRUE ABOUT YOU. MANY TIMES WE´RE AROUND SMALL THINKING PEOPLE SO WE DON´T GROW. CHANGE **YOUR** ENVIRONMENT AND WATCH **YOUR** GROWTH.

Can you relate?

But there is hope. You can get unstuck from your financial situation, just as I did. You can define your own American Dream. I won't say it is easy or even quick, but I will say it is fulfilling and exhilarating.

So, let's take a look at all the mistakes I have made trying to achieve the American Dream. Then I will show you how I created my own American Dream and started living it.

CHAPTER 2

COLLEGES 101

I believe colleges provide negative ROI (Return On Investment). My College education did not help me to get to where I am right now. College failed me: The education that college gave me, failed me. I had to take the future into my own hands in order to actually get somewhere in establishing my career.

So let's take a look at colleges right now, since everyone seems to agree that we need a college degree to get the American Dream we talked about earlier. The cost you pay for a college education may be, for example, $40,000 a year, $60,000, $100,000 or whatever, and the difference between that and how much more money you're actually going to make would be your ROI.

Hypothetically, if you invested $40,000 a year to get a bachelor's degree, your total investment would be $160,000. If you were making $15 per hour, and after getting the degree you started making $22 per hour, that means that after spending $160,000 you have generated an extra

YOU MISS 100% OF THE SHOTS YOU DON'T TAKE

WE SCHOOL OUR CHILDREN IN HISTORY, MATHEMATICS, AND LANGUAGE, BUT NOT IN HAPPINESS, STRENGTH, AND HEALTH - THE MOST IMPORTANT VALUES OF LIFE ITSELF!

$7 per hour. Since you work for only 40 hours per week, that would be an increase of $1,120 per month or $13,440 per year. That means it will take you 12 years to pay off the original debt using all the added income.

Bear in mind that I am not even counting taxes that you will pay on that extra income, so you will actually make even less than that, and it will take a little longer to completely pay off the student loan, too. Also, there is the interest on the student loan debt that will be accumulating, as well. Finally — assuming you get the higher-paying job and you are able to keep it for the next 12 years — after all that, the company that is giving you the $22 hourly job will be trying its best to reduce their expenses, outsource and pay as low an income as possible to their employees, including you.

You need to start looking at colleges as if they are businesses selling degrees and jobs. When you look at it this way, it will help you understand better. You see, colleges and universities exist to make money; even the supposedly not-for-profit colleges also make money. So degrees are products actually created to lure people in. Thus, colleges actually don't need marketing. Your parents and society are the best marketing they already own. Every now and then colleges often do advertise to gain more clients (students). How? Well, you can easily see it a lot of billboards when you ride buses or take the subway. You know the ones that frequently promise something like, "99.9% of our graduates get a job."

That may be true, but where might those jobs be? McDonald's? A car wash? Did your parents or anyone else do their due diligence on finding out who was asked about those jobs? When? Did they verify the graduates' positions, titles, or firms they work at? Did they certify how much the graduates earn? Was the company doing the research also reputable and trustworthy, or was the research done by the college or university itself?

Was the data later on verified by a secondary

source (bear in mind that education hasn't changed much in the past 70 years or so)?

Whatever such advertisements promise, they are probably what swayed your parents, since they are most likely the ones pushing you to get a degree. They are without a doubt the ones who persuaded you to let them invest their money in your higher education or helped you take out loans so you could study, get the degree, and finally get a decent job — and you could then finally move out, and giving them a little peace of mind. Obviously, your parents are going to be upset more than anyone else when it turns out that the traditional American Dream no longer works, especially for you.

Colleges will actually create anything to lure you in so they can get your big bucks for their 'product or service'. A great example occurred when the gaming industry became popular. Remember 'back in the day,' when you were playing video games and telling your parents you just wanted to play video games all day long, every day? The response you always got was, "No, you need to go to college." And that was that, end of conversation.

But now there are gamers, gaming 'Ninjas,' who make a million dollars a year playing video games in the gaming industry, which is fascinating.

IF YOU WANT SOMETHING YOU'VE NEVER HAD THEN YOU'VE GOT TO DO SOMETHING YOU'VE NEVER DONE.

CHANGE YOUR FOCUS, FROM MAKING MONEY TO SERVING MORE PEOPLE. SERVING MORE PEOPLE MAKES THE MONEY COME IN.

There are many video games and even quite a few video game betting companies, sponsors, technical gear, and everything else. Because such a huge vibe was created about gaming and because so many people wanted it, colleges have even created video gaming degrees. You can actually send your kids to college for a bachelor's in gaming: gaming management, arts of gaming, game development, etc. — anything to do with video gaming. Why? Because people wanted it and would pay for it. These days, education is a money-and-jobs enterprise.

When there is a demand from enough people, all you have to do is just fulfill the need, and pretty soon you're in a profitable business. Colleges don't care if people don't actually have enough money to take their courses. They can sign you up for student loans, scholarships, government grants, etc. So it's almost like, "We're going to make sure to put enough loans in your name so you're paying until you're dead." Whether you get a job or not, whether you're successful or not, they don't care. They got their money selling you a product that you cannot even return, in exchange for bills you cannot ever fully cover. No wonder there are reports of so many people defaulting on their student loan payments!

If the gaming example I gave is not enough, how about Marijuana? Go back a couple of years and imagine trying to tell universities to create a master's degree program in that interesting narcotic weed. People would have laughed at you, the president of the U.S. would have condemned you, and you would most likely have been arrested, since Marijuana was not Politically Correct, then.

But the moment Marijuana becomes legal, the moment it becomes Politically Correct and the social norm, that's the moment when colleges and universities will offer degrees in it, with courses about how to grow it, market it, and manage it as a business.

By the way, did you know that today you can earn both a bachelor's and a master's degree in medical biology in several different states — which is pretty much the study of marijuana? And, of course, those colleges are going to help you get all the loans, grants, and scholarships you need to pay for those degrees. Anything that becomes popular, colleges will create a degree for it and lure people in.

My next example will most probably make you laugh and will make you feel the same way as it was a couple of years back when the extreme was not the norm: Prostitution.

Sounds funny to us right now, but people in the recent past would have laughed at you if you had suggested a medical biology degree (study of Marijuana) during the War on Drugs period. However, I believe that the moment prostitution becomes legal that colleges will be offering master's degrees in prostitution, or they would name it something fancier, such as, Managing Multiple Extra-Marital Relationships.

You may cringe at the idea, but to help you understand that colleges/schools are businesses, you can simply take a look at countries where prostitution is legal: Spain, for example. They have at least one school for prostitutes. Don't believe me? Google it for yourself.

Look, a lot of companies are dropping college degree requirements for jobs, as well. Take a look at Elon Musk of Tesla, the electric car manufacturer. He doesn't care if you have a degree or not; he simply cares whether you have the talent to do a job, such as being an accountant for him.

SUCCESS IS NOT GIVEN, IT'S EARNED.

STOP WASTING YOUR LIFE

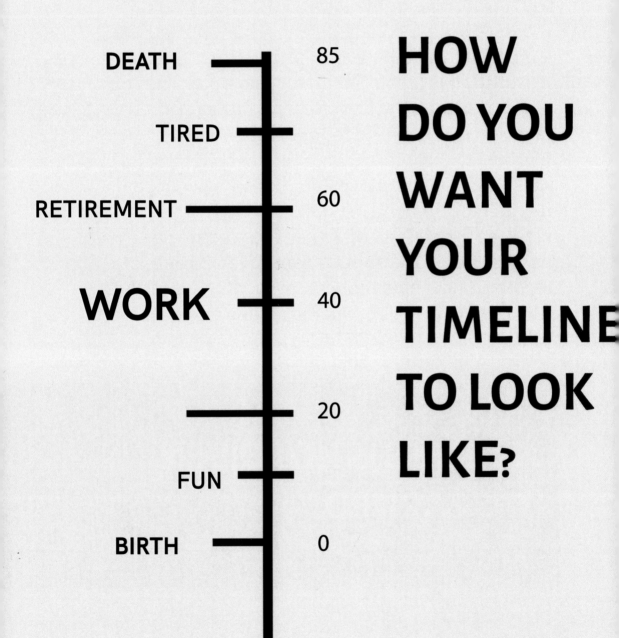

DEATH — 85

TIRED —

RETIREMENT — 60

WORK — 40

— 20

FUN —

BIRTH — 0

HOW DO YOU WANT YOUR TIMELINE TO LOOK LIKE?

Why does he need for you to come in with a bachelor's in accounting if he knows you can use QuickBooks, and with that you can do the whole job? Elon Musk is smart, and he hires based simply on talent.

And then there's Earnest Young, a jobs-consulting company that has dropped its master's degree as a requirement from some career postings. Some other companies have removed the MBA program requirement for hiring employees, because there wasn't any correlation to investing in people's degrees when compared to profits they did or didn't bring companies.

Furthermore, since we are talking about education, let's consider this: The moment you go to college, the next year your knowledge can be obsolete. All textbooks are now the newest edition, so you can't even sell your last year's expensive textbook.

Textbooks have new chapters, new designs, and new everything else, which means your knowledge is a year old. And by the time you finish your theory studies, you will enter the workforce, and your first on-the-job manager will tell you to forget everything you learned in school. Then he will tell you how you are going to be doing the several tasks that make up your job.

So the only thing your degree proves is that you are willing to work for minimum wage for the next four years or so, and you will not complain about anything for at least that long. You will not ask for a raise, you will not ask for anything, and you're simply going to be a very good employee, learning all about the latest techniques and strategies for your job. So a college degree does not guarantee results, and, as I see it, college puts a lot of unnecessary debt and financial pressure on people.

Here's another example: I interviewed a girl for a Relationship Manager position at my company.

As we talked, it became clear that she was about to graduate with a master's degree in marketing. I said, "Wow! Why did you pick marketing?" The conversation continued with a spark of passion. She said it was always her passion to be a marketer, so she studied hard, got along with her professors, and she built a strong rapport with me.

At the end of the interview, I pointed out that she is interviewing with our company because of one of two options: "Either you're willing to sacrifice your dream, your passion, for a steady paycheck to work for me, or you're going to use me as a steppingstone just to get experience, after I put in so much time and money into training you. Then you'll quit when a better opportunity arrives.

POWER OF PERSISTENCE

A RIVER CUTS THROUGH ROCK NOT BECAUSE OF POWER BUT BECAUSE OF ITS PERSISTENCE

Which one of those two options, or is there a third one? If so, please tell me."

Hiring someone for a position that they do not enjoy would be terrible for them and for that employer. They would hate waking up every morning to go to work doing something they do not really enjoy. We can teach the skills, provide the tools, and invest time and money to train and make people successful, but we cannot teach or give them passion for their jobs.

CHAPTER 3

HOUSING TRAP

The second major trap I see for the traditional American Dream is housing.

When people buy their first homes, many actually do themselves more damage than good. When they finally finish their bachelor or master degrees, they seek out the best-paying jobs. As they start receiving their long-awaited, nice juicy salaries, they end up getting the house they always wanted, but can barely afford. Now what happens? For the next thirty years, such people are going to be the most obedient employees.

To protect their dream homes, they will not relocate to other areas, and they will never be late to work, either. They will always comply with exactly what their employer wants, no matter what, because they will be afraid of losing that lovely income that protects the bloated mortgage in their barely viable financial name. They have those expensive, never-ending student loans on top of that, as well. So for the next thirty years, they are going to stay glued to the company that made their home-owning dreams come true.

If there are opportunities to move up in their company by moving to another state, they are quite likely to decline. They might think to rent their dream house out, but since they are going to be landlords, now if something serious happens with their house they will have to book a flight and travel back and forth to handle all kinds of problems — all for practically nonexistent income from their too-beloved house of their dreams.

They may try to sell their dream house, but how long is the house going to sit out there on the market —maybe two, three, or five years? So housing can actually lock you into something less than the American Dream.

Now, why is housing the only thing we actually consider investing in? Because that's the only thing that most people know about. It's just like when you were a child about five years old, and you were asked what do you want to be when you grow up. There are only four or five answers kids usually pick: a doctor, a policeman, a fireman, an astronaut, or a super hero. Since that's what a kids are constantly surrounded by, then those are the choices they are limited to, the roles they will probably choose.

THE DAY YOU PLANT THE SEED IS NOT THE DAY YOU EAT THE FRUIT.

So if you ask any adult, Hey, *how do you want to invest your money?* The answer is almost always, *'Real estate,'* basically the only idea they have heard in their lives. So housing does not help you. In reality, housing actually creates more liabilities than assets for you.

You see, your house is not an asset. Your house is an asset only when it brings you income. When you live in a house, income flows right out of your pocket and away from you. Planning that the value of your house will simply increase over time might be advice you received in the past. However, I know many people who lost an awful lot of money during the housing bubble of 2008. When many mortgages seemed to hover at around $100,000, the value of houses actually went down to about $80,000.

Let's look closer at mortgages. If you have a mortgage on a house, it actually doesn't belong to you: It belongs to the bank. You just simply switched from paying a landlord to paying a bank. Worse, at least if something goes wrong with the house you are renting and living in right now, all that headache belongs to the landlord, including all the expenses involved in fixing the plumbing, repairing the roof, etc. If problems with the rental house are not fixed, you don't have to pay your rent, and you can just move out.

Landlords have to spend time and money to fix problems with their houses, because they can't attract any new tenants and keep their income flowing unless they repair everything.

Yet the moment you take out a mortgage for your dream house, it belongs to the bank, yet all the headaches and expenses for repairs are passed directly on to you.

And if you miss just one mortgage payment, you can say bye-bye to the equity you built, as well as to your credit score. On the other hand, if you were born with a silver spoon in your mouth, or if you work super hard and save enough money to buy real estate for cash, you can either live in the house for free or rent it out to provide yourself a steady flow of income.

But that may not be the best use of your cash. Consider "opportunity loss." Putting X amount of dollars into investment A could prevent you take the same money and put it into investment B. So if the information you have suggests that real estate is the ONLY investment available, you should move forward with that.

THIS NEW GENERATION IS OBSESSED WITH LOOKING SUCCESSFUL INSTEAD OF ACTUALLY BEING SUCCESSFUL.

-KANYE WEST

However, by opening up to other investments and meeting other people, you can learn more ways to make more money than with real estate, just through earning interest, monthly payments, and increased valuation higher than your current rent. This would let you move to a nearby house with better amenities.

Always plan ahead and keep your financial options open. Continuously educate yourself. Don't jump into financial situations unless you fully know what you are doing. As part of your wider education about financial possibilities, if you haven't already read the book, *Rich Dad, Poor Dad* by Robert Kiyosaki and Sharon Letcher, I highly recommend you do so.

SCHOOL WILL NEVER TEACH YOU...

1. **HOW TO SELL**
2. **HOW TO THINK**
3. **HOT TO NEGOTIATE**
4. **HOW TO READ PEOPLE**
5. **HOW TO MANAGE TIME**
6. **HOW TO HANDLE FAILURES**
7. **HOW TO FIND YOUR PASSION**
9. **HOW TO COMMUNICATE WELL**
10. **HOW TO HANDLE INCOME TAX**
11. **HOW TO START A REAL BUSINESS**

CHAPTER 4

RAT RACE

Personally, whenever I think about the traditional American Dream that society and my parents have drilled into my head, I actually look at it as a 40-40-40 formula. The American Dream tells me that I'm going to get a good-paying job, work for 40 hours a week for 40 years of my life, and retire on 40% of my earned income — which is called Social Security.

I'm not sure about you, but I checked my Social Security retirement benefits. If you haven't done so yet, go to *SSA.gov* and take a look to see just how much income you are actually going to receive when you retire, based on what you think your income will probably be over the next thirty to forty years. If you think of all the probable expenses, such as medications, vacations, hospitalizations, your kids (when they have families of their own) asking for help with grandchildren or house purchases, likely emergencies and accidents, as well as your probable retirement program with your company and your 401K program, you will see that you really can't survive with Social Security plus all of that. But that is what you're probably going to get, plain and simple. So if this does not work for you, then why would you subject yourself to that dull and disgusting formula?

Just why are you waking up daily at 6-7 AM, dressing and eating, brushing your teeth, doing your 'toilette,' and shoving a sandwich down your throat so you could spend one hour in traffic going to work and then coming home from work later — to do something you don't really enjoy?

Why not try something new? The answer is fairly simple — because you know nothing better, and nothing new has been given, proposed, or taught to you. No new norms have been created for us that work for today's age.

We simply live by the social pressures and stereotypes that have been 'out there' for about the past 50-80 years. Yet I don't see people still using the mailboxes to mail their letters — they're using email. So long as we're innovating, we need to change expectations and our mindset about the American Dream. That's pretty much what I did.

GOOD PLAYERS WORKOUT, GREAT PLAYERS OUTWORK.

SECTION 1. Chapter 4. Rat Race

"IF YOU WANT TO LOOK GOOD IN FRONT OF THOUSANDS, YOU HAVE TO OUTWORK THOUSANDS IN FRONT OF NOBODY."

-DAMIAN LILLARD

CHAPTER 5

RISK-AVERSE MINDSET

I wanted to grow professionally, financially, and personally. I was ready to invest time and money into myself to increase my own value.

But how are we supposed to grow in today's society when we all have become so risk averse?

Just remember when you were born: You were making every single mistake there is. You tried to walk, you fell, and you tried again until you got it right. You hit your head on every corner. But you learned from all those mistakes. If not, you hit your head a couple more times here and there until you did learn to avoid that. As time progressed, you stopped making all those mistakes and misjudgments.

After all that, what happened to you?

I personally believe that parenting, society, and schooling has made us risk averse. How? Just take a second and recall your kindergarten and elementary school classes. *Don't make this or that mistake; you cannot get an F. Look at your friends right there: They are getting straight A's. You cannot experiment; this is the wrong way of doing it, because you cannot try new things.* Yet adults all agree that we learn differently. Some people are more hands on, while others are bookworms, and there are also passive observers, etc.

WHEN A CHILD LEARNS TO WALK AND FALLS DOWN 50 TIMES, HE NEVER THINKS

TO HIMSELF: "MAYBE THIS ISN'T FOR ME?"

Be a good boy, be a good girl, be completely risk averse — this is how we should *NOT* be doing things. At this particular point, that mindset eliminates what actually makes up an important part of us: taking risks.

If you remove the mindset of taking risks, then you already understand that it will be so much harder to become an entrepreneur, if you want to take your future into your own hands.
So being risk-averse is actually extremely bad. And we need to be able to bring back the opportunity that we gave to our kids, or we give to other people, instead of just laughing about it. We actually should want to tell them, *Hey, you know what? It's okay to make mistakes, its okay to learn from that. It's okay to fail many time as long as you learn from it.* (Just to let you know, I'm going to discuss with you the time/money multiplier formula in later chapters, here. The combination of that formula, as well as working with our failures, is extremely powerful and extremely important to our success in life.)

If we want to grow from our mistakes, then perhaps instead of punishing people for making them, we should actually encourage people to make as many mistakes as quickly as possible, as long as we're learning from them, improving and going forward.

SECTION 1. Chapter 5. Risk-averse mindset

Now a lot of times people say: "Yes, learn from other people's mistakes," but, unfortunately, it doesn't always work that way. You actually learn the best only from your own mistakes. Also you learn quicker, and you move forward faster in that way.

FAIL FAST.

FAIL FORWARD.

FAIL OFTEN.

CHAPTER 6

FAILING FORWARD

Now, we understand that mistakes in life are important, but we need to learn from them by failing *forward*. How can this help you with your push towards your own version of the American Dream? How do we actually remove the mindset of being risk averse that has been socially implanted in us?

Well, I will tell you that it will not happen overnight, as you need to practice. However, there is a trick that I personally like to use.

Remember what we all learned in school about scientific theories? That's what I used to move beyond my own comfort zone — to be continually on the lookout to learn new things, to experiment, to find the unknown.

Remember when we were kids, and we all were trying or experimenting with different things? Then, once we hit middle school and high school, do you remember that making mistakes became a socially embarrassing thing, with everybody else laughing at us?

We decided we didn't want to look like fools.

We started being scared of being judged by others and of doing the wrong thing, of going the wrong way. We didn't want to be left behind and isolated. We began allowing others' opinions and judgments to shape our lives, to define our comfort zones, to restrict our ability of enjoying new things through experimentation.

Again, look at the past.

A parent will always love a child no matter what, no matter how long it actually takes them to 'get it,' to learn something, as long as they do eventually learn. It may have taken you a year longer to learn how to read or how to walk, but you are there now.

Everyone learns at their own pace. And people actually end up learning a lot more by making mistakes than those who stick to traveling the safe road, the safe side of everything.

Simply put, you can always be scared.

You can always sit in your own comfort zone.

LIFE IS HARD FOR TWO REASONS: BECAUSE YOU'RE LEAVING YOUR COMFORT ZONE OR BECAUSE YOU'RE STAYING IN IT.

"I HAVE NOT FAILED. I'VE JUST FOUND 10,000 WAYS THAT WON'T WORK."

-THOMAS EDISON

You can avoid trying new things because you are afraid of looking like a fool, as others judge you and force their opinions on you. Or you can step out and put on your mad scientist white lab coat.

Try new things and learn from them. Then try again and fail again. Fail as many times as needed. Do not let others inflict on you their risk-averse mentality and ruin your fun. If they want to sit at home and do nothing and constantly complain, that's their life choice. You, on the other hand, can take life into your own hands. You can step out into the unknown.

You will be full of excitement, since gathering new information is fun, even if it involves failure. But just remember to fail correctly.

What do I mean, *fail correctly?* Remember that I treat leaving my comfort zone as a scientist gathering data. I document everything, learn from it and try to set up different experiments with the data I've gained. So it gets really easy and painless when you start thinking of everything as a science experiment.

Sending 1000 emails out with your resume is easy. Document the findings and results. No interview? What is the new theory? Perhaps the subject could be adjusted a bit. Try a new subject and send 1000 more emails? What are the results? Experimenting and documenting your failures will let you see the truth and help you grow faster, while eliminating fear of failure.

Remember, you didn't fail — you just gathered data and information. And you have successfully acquired some very valuable information. Because of that, you are much closer to the solution when compared to a person who does not have that data. Failure should be your greatest teacher.

The lessons failure will give you are not

exactly free. You pay for them. And the currency you use is time.

You have to remember that time is the only currency that you can convert into anything. You can convert time to connections, money and knowledge, but nothing converts backwards. That is, money will not buy you more time. It is a finite resource that you possess, and it is constantly running out. Every time you go out, experiment, try new things and gather valuable data, you pay with time.

Remember that knowledge costs you X amount of time. That means that you just became an investor in time. You invest your limited time to learn something, to exchange it for money, to build new connections. Realize the high importance of time and how you use it or waste it. Once you do, it will help you grow further and faster. Spend time reading books instead of watching a wonderful new Netflix Series. Spend time going to conferences instead of sitting in a bar. Spend or invest your time wisely, and the dividends will keep multiplying forever.

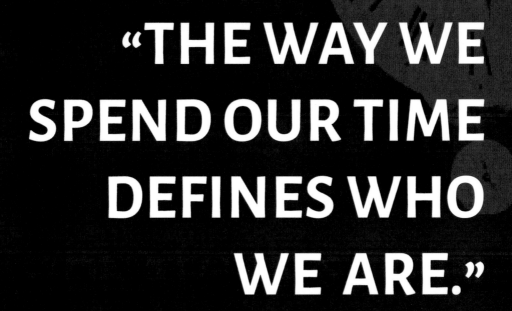

"THE WAY WE SPEND OUR TIME DEFINES WHO WE ARE."

-JONATHAN ESTRIN

SUMMARY OF SECTION 1

If you are looking for an education such as a college degree in business management or finance, it would be better instead to concentrate on finding a good mentor.
Use the money that you or your parents would spend on college and pay it to your mentor directly. There are even a lot of mentors who are willing to teach you free of charge.

Just think for a second. You could send a message to a CEO or a partner from a boutique Wall Street firm and say something about his line of work has always been your dream, your goal. You want to do what he does as a profession for the rest of your life. You are so serious about it that you will work days as well as nights for him for free to learn everything from A to Z about his profession for the next four years. You will learn from all the staff and all the employees, and all the third parties involved. You will master their software and their other tools.

You will learn and understand that business

inside and out.

At the end of the mentorship, if the CEO will not give you a position, he/she would be very stupid. Why let go of an asset that has been loyal to you, worked for you, has been trained by you, and can be put to use immediately. If they will not give you an offer, their competitor will in a second, simply because of how much you know and who you know.

So don't be trapped in the 9-to-5 business rat race. There shouldn't be a rule that when you work five days, you should relax for two. You should relax when you need to relax and then work the rest. Tired? Take a break. All good? Continue where you left off. As Gary Vaynerchuk said: "If you live for weekends and vacations, your life is broken."

Your paycheck can be like a drug, and you can be addicted. Just like a drug, you can get hooked on it, and it can be hard to live without. You can experience the symptoms of euphoria when that direct deposit hits your bank account, and you can experience stress and uneasiness when you don't. Just

SECTION 1. Summary of section 1

like a drug, the euphoria you experience when you get your paycheck usually lasts long enough to get you to the next 'dose.' Just like a drug, you always want more checks, and it makes you happy when your check gets bigger, just like the larger dosage in a drug. Understand it, and break free from it, by learning how to fail in your free time.

Learn to love making mistakes. Use them to your advantage to move forward. Remember, in order to make good decisions in life, you need experience. You gain experience by making bad decisions. It is that simple. If you want to grow, you need to find a way to be able to make those bad decisions, make those mistakes, and fail in peace without being judged by others. Greatness and true success were never born by sitting in a comfort zone.

Finally, monitor your time and how you invest it. If you remember, we spoke about 'opportunity loss' on investment, when for every minute you invest being sad, you lose an opportunity to invest 60 seconds in being happy.

We all have 24 hours available to each of us. How and where you invest your 24 hours is up to you.

"HE WHO WORKS ALL DAY, HAS NO TIME TO MAKE MONEY."

-JOHN ROCKEFELLER

SECTION2.

CHAPTER 7

24-HOUR CEO

So how did I grow professionally and personally so fast? I worked harder and longer than anyone else.

I built a fast-growing financial services company that achieved 4600% growth between 2016 and 2020. In fact, it was recognized as an Inc. 5000 company. In 2019, my company was ranked #64.

My company made the Entrepreneur 360 list in 2016, 2018, and 2019.

I was also recognized during the NBA Hall of Fame game by Dr. J as *Entrepreneur of the Year* in 2019.

I have mentored over a dozen people to financial independence and security. Some have gone on to make millions.

Because I worked so hard, I went from a high school graduate to holding a masters-degree in 3 years.

I am a Self-Made Millionaire — no millionaire daddy, no loans from rich friends. It was all just me working as hard as I could all the time.

I also realized that I was constantly being risk averse, and I understood that I actually needed to make mistakes.

Those are the basics, the important foundation I needed in order to establish my business,' LIFE CORP'.

And I pretty much started to run my own life as a business.

Now, I know a lot of people look up to millionaires and billionaires such as Jeff Bezos or Mark Zuckerberg.

I admire and learn from companies like Amazon and Facebook. **Successful businesses offer more lessons than individuals. It is much easier to study the success of a company than an individual. You can dig into their financial, marketing, R&D and other public aspects of a company.** With that in mind, I started learning how to run my life more and more like a business.

As I learned more about businesses, their structures, policies, material, resources, and their financials, I was able to put what I learned to use right away. Instead of using the information for the business, I used all the material and knowledge for my personal life. So pretty much what I'm talking about is, you should run your life like a business, *completely.*

The only difference between your life and your business is that businesses invest money, their biggest resource, right?

BEING BROKE IS PART OF THE JOURNEY. STAYING BROKE IS A FUCKING CHOICE.

IF YOU'RE NOT WHERE YOU WANNA BE IN YOUR LIFE, WHY YOU CHILLING SO MUCH?

Well the biggest personal resource we have for our lives is time, which is equivalent to money and is often considered to be more valuable. So we can invest money or time, and run our life like business in order to move forward.

You need to have accountability. You need to learn how to run your life like a business, efficiently and ethically, without losing any of your assets. Keep an eye on your competitors and make sure your shareholders are happy. Businesses would hate it if a couple of million dollars were lost, right? If you run your life as a business, your money equivalent is time, as I pointed out. Now, I don't see people hating themselves when two or three hours leaks completely out of their lives. Again, start looking at time as a resource for your 'life business' in order to invest and grow. You need to have budgeting set up in order to analyze and evaluate correctly. But more on that later.
You see, every person has a limited amount of resources, time, and money. Just like any other business, there is no one right way to run a business. Everyone runs at their own pace, with their own philosophy of what they believe. But as long as you understand that your life is a business, you're actually able to clean it up and grow much faster.

This is exactly what allowed me to get married to the love of my life after just three months of dating, and we are happily married for ten years and counting.

Again, I'm treating my life as a business with laser-focused concentration. I am the CEO of my life, and I get to decide how things will move forward. As a CEO, I will need to make a lot of hard, and challenging decisions.

So where do you start? What is the first thing that you need to do? Just like any business, you need to correctly set up all of the needed departments of your business.

GROWTH & COMFORT DO NOT COEXIST

-GINNY ROMETTI

CHAPTER 8

HUMAN RESOURCES DEPARTMENT

Can the CEO pick the board of directors? No. The board of directors picks the CEO. When you take a look at the Yahoo board of directors hiring the CEO, they basically told him the following: "Hey, this is what you need to do, okay? You need to make more money for our shareholders, you need to do this, you need to do that."

A board of directors tells a CEO what to do, and the CEO brings in their own network, connections, resources, ideas, etc. The CEO can never fire a member of the board of directors. Now, if you treat your life as a business, and you are the CEO, then who is your board of directors that you can never fire? Your family: your parents, your father, mother, spouse, kids, etc. They are on the board. They are directors. They can dictate what they want out of me, and I cannot fire them.

So it's very important to understand who is on your board of directors, and who has the most influence. Then you also have a board of advisors. As the CEO, you appoint people to your board of advisors.

But you want to be very careful who you actually bring onto your advisory board. You don't want to bring just anyone. So if we're talking about business, you usually concentrate on bringing attorneys, investors, people with a lot of connections, or a lot of money and a lot of influence. In your personal life, your current advisory board consists of people who are currently giving you advice. And so, what are they bringing to your 'business'? Problems? Headaches? More work?

What kind of accomplishments do they have? What qualifies them to even be on your advisory board?

Would you take advice from a lazy neighbor on how to get a six-pack? No one would, right? So why do you take advice from your parents? From society? From a friend, on how to be happy or rich, if they, themselves, are miserable and broke?

Personally, I would want to take advice from somebody who is actually happy, who is making money, and who is knowledgeable and successful. Those are the people that you want to bring onto your advisory board, right? And where do you find them?

Let's say you are interested in real estate, and you are looking for successful people to bring to your advisory board. I would advise you to start with books on real estate. Reading books on real estate is like listening to an expert, to begin with. Pick up a book on real estate topics. Such a simple move, and you have already added experts to your advisory board.

NEVER TAKE ADVICE FROM SOMEONE WHO ISN'T IN THE SAME POSITION YOU WANT TO BE.

TEN YEARS FROM NOW, MAKE SURE YOU CAN SAY THAT YOU CHOSE YOUR LIFE, YOU DIDN'T SETTLE FOR IT.

Next, go to YouTube and find some real estate channels out there. Ask questions, post comments. Listen to podcasts. Go to real estate meetups, conferences, and events. You will meet a lot of people on that topic, people who are interested in the same topic.

Don't forget you can literally DM (direct message) anyone *right now* on Instagram and ask them for advice, ask them for their opinion. And guess what? A lot of people will respond and will provide the advice you need. Again, there are a lot of people that you can bring onto your advisory board who will bring their experience, network, passion, and sometimes even resources.

Besides a board of directors and a board of advisors, you also need employees, of course. Now, I believe a company is as good as its people. You bring in bad employees, and your company is going down. Bring in cancer into your business, your world, and it simply spreads. You may have one person who works for your organization who is completely unhappy, complaining, bitching, etc. It's going to spread, and they're going to gossip to somebody else, and then you have at least two or more people who are not happy.

You have to eliminate cancer right away. People have to enjoy what they're doing, and you want to bring in the best of the best to your company, which is how every company grows. Without good, talented, happy employees, there is no growth, there is nothing good.

It's the same thing in life: Your employees are the people you surround yourself with, your friends, your co-workers, and the like. Now think, which of those employees will be helping your business move forward? And which of those employees are stealing from you? What are they stealing? To start with, one of your most important assets: they could easily be stealing your time. They're the ones who are dragging you to bars, the ones who are constantly complaining, those who are constantly asking you to watch some new online series, those who are constantly recommending something that will be negatively impacting your 'business.'

You want to bring in employees who will positively impact your business. They would say, *Hey, you know what? Let's go to this meetup event, let's go over here. Let's watch this documentary; I believe this is a good article; you should read it.*
Such people will bring new knowledge to your business and introduce you to people you want to meet and who will support you mentally and financially in your time of need.

So then it is time for cleanup. I told you earlier you will have to make some drastic and hard decisions. You will probably have some people

"NEVER DISCOURAGE ANYONE WHO CONTINUALLY MAKES PROGRESS, NO MATTER HOW SLOW."

-PLATO

YOU WOULDN'T LET ASSHOLES LIVE IN YOUR HOUSE - WHY LET THEM LIVE IN YOUR HEAD?

who will be dragging you down or stealing your time. It is time to fire everyone who is negatively impacting your business, literally fire them. No hard feelings; it's just business. You need to move forward, and you cannot allow your business to be dragged down by bad employees.

I did that in my life. I fired them. I stopped talking to everybody who was negative or not valuable. I eliminated all forms of contact with them — not online, not in person, no texting, nothing. It sounds tough and a hard move, but I needed to move forward, I needed to grow, I needed to find solutions. I would not let anything or anybody hold me back.

I removed everybody from my high school days, from my college days, from my past work, past dates. I needed to be positioned correctly. Then I hired new employees to my life, and they actually brought a lot of positive impact to push me and the business forward.

Again, where will you find them? I mentioned it earlier. If you are interested in marketing, and you want to organize your business in marketing, look for people with similar interests or people who compliment that type of business. If you're in music, go to places where a lot of people who love music are and network and build new friends there.

You need people who are actually successful in your points of interest, and you can ask them for advice. You can bring them onto your advisory board, or you can just become friends. Again, it's actually better for you to talk to people who are also as passionate about the topic as you are. As you restructure your human resources department, it is important to first eliminate cancer, then hire. Why? If you leave even a single negative person and bring in ten new people, the new people could easily be affected by the negative one.

I personally went to extremes on this topic, and it has helped me. I kind of disappeared for three years. I legally changed my name and my Social Security number. I started my life, my 'business,' all over again, from zero. This time, I was really careful about who I was associating with and who I brought into my life. I networked and hung out with millionaires, people who were much older than me. I asked them questions, and I was interested in their businesses and in contributing to them, as well. I brought them to my life as mentors. For example, Jacob Shimon and Vlad Sadovskiy were kind enough to give me their time and provide educational resources.

Remember, any relationship is a two-way street. If you are only taking info and not providing anything in return, that makes you a leech and not a friend.

WHO ARE YOUR FRIENDS?

YOU BECOME WHO YOU HANG WITH

I read *The Wall Street Journal, The New York Times*, and I signed up on various forums to get information that I could read and contribute and share with people that I started associating with. I listened to their recommendations, their book suggestions, and their ideas. I hung out with like-minded entrepreneurs, go-getters, tinkerers, doers. I surrounded myself with positive thinkers and put myself on a strong motivational diet.

I listened to podcasts from Gary Vanerchuk during tough times, and it always helped me get up and push forward. I stopped taking advice from people who are not experts. And finally I was able to create my perfect Human Resources department that works for me, my dreams, and my ideas.

CHAPTER 9

MARKETING DEPARTMENT

It is time to move forward and establish a marketing department in the 'business' of your life.

Believe it or not, people do judge by 'covers' or by first impressions. This is why you need to have a strong marketing department. Anywhere you go, for example, a supermarket, you will see that the package perfectly located with a nice design and cover is what's going to catch your eye.

That's product placement and design. Or perhaps you are going to pick up something that you always have bought or there is a brand you trust. Sometimes your friends may recommend what product you should buy.

Look, the entire marketing department of your business is extremely important, and you will need to work on it. I doubt you will shop at the store that smells like piss. How about buying a car from the dealer who has a super bad reputation? There is always room for improvements and development, but first you need to realize that you are the product that is being marketed to buyers.

So what kind of marketing are businesses using? Let's start with flyers and packaging. For you, it's the clothing that you wear, the way you talk, your mannerism, your smell. I remember that I had a mirror sticker that made my mirror look like the cover of Forbes magazine. Right before I leave my house, I always look at myself in the mirror and say, *Is this the day that they will take pictures of me, and is this how I will be remembered?* When I got married, my wife threw out 90% of all my clothing. We went shopping, and even now if you inspect my closet you will only find dress shirts and suits. And I personally own only one pair of jeans and one pair of sweatpants, for the gym.

Now, I am not saying throw away all your clothing and buy only suits. I did it to myself because I believe luck is defined when opportunity meets your preparation. And I always have to be ready and prepared.

YOUR SALARY IS THE BRIBE THEY GIVE YOU TO FORGET YOUR DREAMS.

At the end of the day, you're only able to do a first impression once, and you have to make sure it counts. What I am saying is that you should buy the style of clothing that targets and speaks to your buyers. If you want to hang out with investment bankers, I doubt appearing with green hair, ripped jeans, and a butterfly tattoo on your left cheek will help you break the ice and join the circle. It may be possible, but your chances would probably be lessened simply because of the marketing and product packaging you picked.

You might be surprised, but you are building your reputation and your brand daily. All of your actions (and sometimes lack of actions) are responsible for how people define you when you are not in the room.

We all have examples when someone calls us and we don't pick up. Or we hang up on someone every now and then. I have been guilty of that, but these actions slowly build your 'brand.'

Let's take a look at an example. You had a bad experience with your cell phone provider. They overcharged you. So you call that 800 number and you yell at them, and there is no way they can just simply ignore you. You know it, they know it. They know they made a mistake, and they know you are the paying customer so they let you vent. They can't hide. They can't drop the call on you. If you are running your life as a business, you need

"MONDAY DOESN'T SUCK.
THE WEATHER DOESN'T SUCK.
YOUR JOB DOESN'T SUCK.

YOUR NEGATIVE
MINDSET SUCKS.

YOUR LACK OF
SELF-WORTH AND
SELF LOVE SUCKS"

-JIM CARREY

to take it seriously . No more hiding. Accept your mistakes, apologize, and try to improve and grow from it.

Here's another example: I always hate when I have to call to set up my internet provider, and they tell me that a technician will arrive anytime between the hours of 12 and 4. If they don't show up at all, I will be livid because I lost four hours of my valuable time. When you don't show up on time, that's the brand you are creating. If you are often late, or you don't show up at meetings, you are simply building a non-reliable brand. I know I will never count on you to do anything or trust you with getting to meetings. My point is that if you hate when it is done to you, don't do that type of thing to others — the Golden Rule, right?

WE ALL HAVE 24 HOURS A DAY, SUCCESSFUL PEOPLE USE IT AND THE LOSERS WILL ABUSE IT.

We are all quick to jump on the computer and start writing negative reviews about our experiences. Or we spend two hours on hold to reach a corporate office to complain. People simply do not go to such lengths to provide positive feedback. It is much harder to earn recognition these days, yet it takes only a second for a negative review. If you run your life as a business, your marketing department needs to go above and beyond, every day and all the time.

CHAPTER 10

SALES DEPARTMENT

Every company out there is selling some kind of product or service. There are automotive companies selling cars, which are products, or there are attorneys selling legal knowledge, which is service. If you are the business yourself, you are selling something, as well. As a matter of fact, you are a natural born sales rep. After you were born, your sales skills improved rapidly over time.

For example, remember when you were 3 months old the way you were selling was by yelling and screaming to get the bottle. Over time, your sales skills improved. You began identifying who to sell to in order to close the deal, thus you began asking just mommy, instead of daddy, for something because daddy always ignored you and always said no.

When you got older, you started giving something of value when you were selling. A good example is when you became a teenager. You cleaned your whole bedroom and took out the garbage — in other words, you generated value up front and prepped for your sale. Then you asked your parents if it would be okay to come home at 10:30 pm, instead of 9:00 pm, later that evening. You were selling to your parents, trying to get them to extend your usual curfew. So as you grew up, you were constantly improving as a sales rep, and then, as we noted earlier, what happened is that you became risk averse.

Becoming risk averse has killed you as a sales rep. It has killed your closing skills and even your pitching skills. However, you should understand that at the end of the day, you are always selling something. A 'sale' is being done when you try to get a girlfriend (you're the better mate or companion), when you talk to friends about going to a certain bar (instead of some other, lesser quality bar), and when you think your decision about something is better (trying to overcome the alternate facts and the reasoning of your friends). Either you will persuade your friends to your point of view, or the opposing party will persuade otherwise. The point is, that you are always trying to make some sort of 'sale,' just like everyone else.

Your sales skills are so important that even when you come to a job interview, you are selling yourself that you are the perfect candidate for the job. So you actually want to improve your sales skills, to become better at it. You need to stop being afraid of possible rejections.
This risk-averse mindset about rejections and failures has ruined the traditional American Dream. It impacts you every day. You need to be prepared to 'fail forward' and learn from negative experiences. Do not be embarrassed about picking up girls in a bar, just because you think your friends are going to laugh at you, or you are going to make a fool of yourself. Remember that, those friends are the 'bad employees' for

"WHEN I WAS 5 YEARS OLD, MY MOTHER ALWAYS TOLD ME THAT HAPPINESS WAS THE KEY TO LIFE. WHEN I WENT TO SCHOOL, THEY ASKED ME WHAT I WANTED TO BE WHEN I GREW UP. I WROTE DOWN "HAPPY". THEY TOLD ME I DIDN'T UNDERSTAND THE ASSIGNMENT, AND I TOLD THEM THEY DIDN'T UNDERSTAND LIFE."

–JOHN LENNON

DO SHARKS COMPLAIN ABOUT MONDAY? NO. THEY'RE UP EARLY, BITING STUFF, CHASING SHIT, BEING SCARY - REMINDING EVERYONE THEY'RE A FUCKING SHARK.

the business of your life. They're supposed to be encouraging you, instead of holding you back.

Thus, to help you grow better as a sales rep of your life, you need to learn more about the product and the services. Then utilize all that knowledge to actually go and sell. Having sales knowledge and sales skills will open up multiple doors for you. With all that, you can make as much money as you want; you can have almost anything you want in life if you are a very good sales rep. So you need to improve your sales department. To help you do that, you need to start collecting and analyzing data whenever you sell. Let's take a look at a couple of examples where data gathering and analysis could be helping you close more deals.

Let's say you are looking for a job, which means you are selling yourself. So you send a hundred resumés for various job openings, and if you don't get a job, you should evaluate the data and try to understand it. *What kind of data?* you might ask. You could begin by looking at the subject title, which you might need to change. Experiment with that, and then send 100 more resumés out. Evaluate the new data. Is it better? Do the emails even get opened? Did you get any new responses? Start building up the sales funnel and try tracking data and understanding your ratios.

If you send 100 emails, most likely only 40 are being opened. If you receive 20 invites for a phone interview, then out of that 20 you might get 5 invites to a second interview. Out of that 5, you might get 1 job offer. So, basically, if you send out 200 emails, realistically speaking, you might get 2 decent interviews. However, you'll want to improve your sales department and get more quality out of your sales process.

You will want to polish your interview skills to get 2 offers out of 5 in-person interviews. Or you might want to get 10 in-person interviews out of 20 phone-call interviews.

The same funnels will work in anything you do. Gathering product knowledge, acquiring data, and experimenting with it will improve your ratios. Furthermore, why not take a look at other successful business practices and what they are doing and how they are selling? Even though many businesses use those techniques, you should feel free to use them as well for your life or whatever you are selling or trying to achieve.

Here's an idea worth considering: All that spam you receive every day, why do you still receive it? Because it works. Instead of deleting it and complaining about it, learn from it. Learn the creative marketing techniques; learn the creative sales pitches; for instance. How do they overcome rebuttals or rejections? Once you learn how to sell, how to overcome rebuttals, everything else is the same, no matter what product you are selling. Gather that info and create your own sales pitch for your product.

Those annoying telemarketers that are calling you nonstop, selling you student loans or car insurance? Pick up the call and listen to their opening line. See how they overcome your rebuttals when you say you are not interested or you say you already have a good rate with their competitor.

BREAKING NEWS: YOU NEED TO HANG OUT WITH PEOPLE WHO FIT YOUR FUTURE NOT YOUR HISTORY

Remember that rejections will always be there. Every single time you're trying to sell something, you're always opening up yourself for an opportunity to be rejected. Your job is to try to improve the odds in your favor so you will be rejected *less.* Whether you're picking up a girl in a bar, asking somebody to marry you, or applying for a job, the chance of rejection is always there.

Don't get the wrong idea: I'm not teaching how to sell. There are hundreds of books for that. But without the sales department, the business will not move forward. Just remember that failures and rejections are a part of sales and thus they are a part of success.

IF YOU THINK YOU ARE TOO SMALL TO MAKE A DIFFERENCE, TRY SLEEPING WITH A MOSQUITO IN THE ROOM.

CHAPTER 11

R&D DEPARTMENT

We have discussed many departments in a business already, and we still have a few left. Every department is important and plays a vital part in your business. Now we'll see how Research and Development (R&D) works in business, as well as in your personal life. To get started, let's take a look at Blockbuster, the video rental business. You don't see them around anymore because they failed to innovate.

Here is a simple reminder that there is always somebody out there who wants success more than you, who is more talented than you. They're working hard to take it away from you. So if you fail to innovate, if you fail to improve, you are not going to move forward. Research and Development is extremely important in analyzing your market, analyzing your skillset, understanding your product better, and improving your products, services, and business skills.

If your life is your business, what should your Research and Development department be doing for you? You could learn to play a musical instrument; you could learn another language. You can learn how to use Excel or a programming language. You can always learn something new. Whatever the job/career you have right now, if you want a higher management position, if you want to move up the ladder, you need to constantly improve yourself. Even if you achieve your current goal, you should continuously improve your skill set to stay competitive. At the end of the day, there is some kid in India who is willing to do your job, and he's way more talented, way more knowledgeable, and willing to work way more for cheaper.

You must understand that there is always a bigger fish out there, that there is another guy out there who's richer, smarter, more talented, better looking, and in love with your wife. You need to improve, innovate, evolve, and adapt in order to maintain your position of advantage and to move forward. You have to maintain a competitive advantage all the time in order to keep your competitive edge. A good offense is the best defense.

So how should your Research and Development department actually work to improve your business? Well, you can spend profitable time on YouTube, for example, as a tool for learning business skills (as long as you use it to improve your business skill set and not simply to watch cute cat videos). Also that great tool called Google can train you in whatever business skills you want to learn for improving your business. Look at your current board of advisors/directors, or even some of your employees, who can help you, teach you, direct you in obtaining whatever business knowledge you desire to develop.

YOUR FIRST PODCAST WILL BE AWFUL.

YOUR FIRST ARTICLE WILL BE AWFUL.

YOUR FIRST ART WILL BE AWFUL.

YOUR FIRST PHOTO WILL BE AWFUL.

YOUR FIRST GAME WILL BE AWFUL.

BUT YOU CAN'T MAKE YOUR 50TH WITHOUT MAKING YOUR FIRST.

SO GET IT OVER WITH, AND
MAKE IT.

NOT SEEING RESULTS?
FEEL LIKE GIVING UP?

CONSIDER THIS: THE LAST THING TO GROW ON A FRUIT TREE...

IS THE FRUIT.

So many businesses fail because they simply fail to innovate and improve. Do not become one of them. Even if you have to learn new skills by spending money, it would be worth it, as you cannot stand still. And your Research and Development department cannot work just by itself. For instance, you need to gather data on your audience from your Marketing Department and feed it to your Sales Department. Your Sales Department should provide data on your successful sales, sales funnels, and failed sales attempts to your Research and Development department.

Research and Development should analyze that data and make suggestions for improving sales tactics, provide suggestions on how to improve the product, and provide information on how to improve marketing. They can start by simply observing how other 'companies' are performing. Again, we are not just going to look at other people, but also other businesses.

For instance, why is a particular business so good at selling? They are gathering data on you, and they know everything about you. Are you gathering data when you sell? Are you gathering data on your employees, on your customers? Most people don't. It is time to learn the most powerful tool: Client Relationship Management (CRM).

Customer Relationship Management software is easily available to pretty much anyone. It collects and organizes data on just about anything you want. For example, you can start collecting information on all your past conversations and organize it neatly. With CRM, you will never forget the name of the spouse of the person you met three month ago. Or where did your co-worker go on vacation three years ago?

It is time to use the same tools and tactics that are available to big businesses in your personal life. Just imagine how your life can improve with stronger relationships, when you remember everything. This data will help you in sales, understanding your audience, understanding your employees, and help you acquire, store, and retrieve whatever data you want. It is time to start collecting information!

There are so many free, personal CRMs that you can use right now. You will start remembering not only people's birthdays, but their anniversaries, as well as other important dates and information that will make your bond, your connection with others, stronger, which makes it so much easier to make a sale when you want to. Developing and deepening all such personal relationships is extremely important. You don't have to reinvent the wheel, just do what other big companies are already doing by collecting useful information.

IF YOU FEEL LIKE YOU'RE LOSING EVERYTHING, REMEMBER THAT TREES LOSE THEIR LEAVES EVERY YEAR AND THEY STILL STAND TALL AND WAIT FOR BETTER DAYS TO COME.

Besides the CRM, other tools are available that will make your life easier, that help big businesses. There are tools to mass email with beautiful templates.

Let's say you are emailing your resumés, and typing them one-by-one would be annoying and time wasting. Just import the data and create a template that will look beautiful when compared to the competition. It will make you stand out from the crowd. You can mass email this and even know if they are being opened or if recipients just click on your online resumé.

If businesses are using Facebook ads to drive their sales, why not use Facebook ads to find a job and make sure that what you add is only visible to recruiters?

1% LUCK
1% TALENT
98% NEVER GIVE UP.
100% SUCCESS FORMULA.

THERE ARE WAY EASIER PLACES TO WORK, BUT NOBODY EVER CHANGED THE WORLD ON 40 HOURS A WEEK.

-ELON MUSK

How about *Fiverr*, where you can quickly outsource your work or get something done for cheap? *Canva* can be your go-to tool for design. *Unsplash* could become your go-to for picture content.

My point is that there are tons of tools that are already developed and used by big corporations that you can just plug-and-play, for your own business. If you're running your life as a business, you need to start using those business tools to start gathering information and data, as well as push your 'business' forward.

If you innovate and improve every day, you will start seeing the difference. With me, for example, overtime helped develop my own brand, and my reputation. I picked up advanced Excel, I learned how to build a website, how to code, a little bit of marketing, and I used a little bit of speed reading. I needed at least basic information on various topics to make sure that, when I am outsourcing something, they will not be able to take advantage of me.

Finally, remember that the greatest tool for innovation is failure. Do not be afraid to go out and try something new. At the end of the day, you will either succeed or gather data for your Research and Development department to help you improve in the future. Your data on failure is extremely important, as you will learn in the following chapters. A lot of people misunderstand that a person who has failed 1000 times trying to do something vs a person who hasn't, is way more valuable, as they possess information that is not easily available. This information (good or bad), this data, can be monetized.

CHAPTER 12

FINANCIAL DEPARTMENT

As you are trying to understand all of the departments of your business and what each needs to be doing, it may start to sound like a lot of work. How much time and money do you need to spend on each? What should you be concentrating on first? Who should be keeping me accountable? The answers to those questions should be with the Financial Department of a business.

Your Financial Department will help you run your 'business' and will keep you on track. What exactly will you be tracking? You will be tracking the Return On Investment (ROI).

Now, big corporations always need to understand if the money they are spending/investing is helping them grow, or, in other words, is the money well spent? Is everything working? Is everything moving forward daily, quarterly, yearly? Companies using money as a tracking tool can easily analyze how much they have invested vs how much they are getting back from the investments.

If you are treating your life as a business, your tracking tool is mainly time. Look back to what we have already covered. We talked about many departments of your business. We talked about the Sales Department actually doing some selling/ pitching. We talked about the Human Resources Department managing and hiring all your

COMFORT IS A DRUG.

ONCE YOU GET USED TO IT, IT BECOMES ADDICTING.

GIVE A WEAK MAN CONSISTENT SEX, GOOD FOOD, CHEAP ENTERTAINMENT, AND HE'LL THROW HIS AMBITIONS RIGHT OUT THE WINDOW.

THE COMFORT ZONE IS WHERE DREAMS GO TO DIE.

employees and making sure they are working, and working efficiently.

We talked about managing your Marketing Department, evaluating, creating your brand, creating a positive value. We talked about Research and Development, spending time online, and investigating and collecting data. Who is tracking all the time that you spend on all of this? Your Financial Department should be tracking all of this.

Here is the interesting part. There is no secret formula that if you have, let's say, 120 – 150 hours per week, then you have put 10 hours in Research and Development, another 40 hours into Sales, 20 hours into Marketing, etc. Every company runs differently, and so should you. Some will spend more time on R&D and less in marketing, or another company may outsource marketing completely and spend those extra hours somewhere else.

The most important factor to understand is that in businesses, once the Financial Department catches someone stealing money or sees that a project does not generate the right returns, the project will be closed or the person responsible will be fired. Since you are investing time, your Financial Department should monitor this as one of the most valuable assets and obviously fire and remove anything that's stealing your time.

WHEN A PHOTOGRAPHER CAN'T CHANGE A SCENE, HE CHANGES HIS ANGLE AND LENS TO CAPTURE THE BEST OF THAT SCENE.

SIMILARLY, WHEN YOU CAN'T CHANGE A SITUATION IN YOUR LIFE, CHANGE YOUR PERSPECTIVE TO GET THE BEST OUT OF THAT SITUATION. TRY TO BE A FILTER, NOT A SPONGE.

Track where your time is actually going; obviously, it should not be spent on Netflix; it should not be spent in bars, unless you're selling something or recruiting someone for your business or researching.

Remember the company that you are running. Your life, at the current moment, has a particular goal. Your financial department should put all the resources, all your time and money, towards achieving that goal, towards acquiring the right skills, towards making connections and network that are useful and needed.

So if you are weak in one department, you have two options. One is to spend valuable time and pick up a book and start learning. Two, spend your time working elsewhere, converting time to money and outsourcing someone who is good in that department. At the end of the day, you will spend time wisely by doing this.

If your Financial Department is on point, then you know where your time is going and where it is being wasted. If you start thinking of your life as a business, you will start noticing this more often. Remember, your time can always be converted into improving your life.

Minutes and hours accumulate. It could be wiser to spend time in one of your departments or just convert it to cash. Make sure that your Financial Department is keeping you accountable, not only to yourself, but also to your board of directors and employees.

SUCCESS ISN'T THE KEY TO HAPPINESS. HAPPINESS IS THE KEY TO SUCCESS. IF YOU LOVE WHAT YOU'RE DOING, YOU'LL BE SUCCESSFUL.

DID YOU KNOW?

NO ONE CAN DESTROY IRON, BUT ITS OWN RUST CAN. LIKEWISE, NO ONE CAN DESTROY A PERSON, BUT HIS OWN MINDSET CAN.

SUMMARY OF SECTION 2

It is time to recognize that you are the CEO of your own life. You are running your life, your 'business' 24/7, and the main resources that are at your disposal are time and money. True, everyone is born under different circumstances and may have better connections or knowledge from the start, or perhaps a bit more money. At the end of the day, we all have the same 24 hours in a day. Your time can be converted to money, connections, knowledge, or pretty much any other resource.

Once you start seeing your life as a business and start organizing your departments correctly, you can achieve unbelievable results. In my case, I run my life as a business with laser-focused concentration, and I was able to — graduate high school in three years; get my bachelor's degree in less than two years; get my master's degree in six months. And I used the same laser-focused concentration on my love life, as well. I found the love of my life and have been happily married for 10 years, after only three months of dating.

Businesses that I started have grown by more than 4400% in merely three years. After becoming an entrepreneur in five years, I learned accounting, book keeping, tax laws, investments, real estate, website building, marketing, cinematography, public speaking, publishing, writing, and speed reading. I have managed to build a personal brand and reputation. I have met various celebrities and shared speaking stages with the likes of: Dr. J, Mario Lopez, Colin Farrell, Sharon Lechter, Kevin Harrington, Les Brown, and many others.

And I want to make sure you understand that these basic principles, this philosophy, can be used in various aspects of your life. So let's put it all together and run some examples.

NOT EVERYDAY WILL BE A GOOD DAY, BUT YOU'LL HAVE TO SHOW UP ANYWAY AND CRUSH IT.

If I were a 17-year-old and would love to make money just playing video games for the rest of my life, I would come to my board of directors (my parents) and tell them that I do not want to go to college for 3-4 years. Instead, I'd tell them that I wanted to build a business and would make money playing video games. It would take me three years to build, and if I fail, I will go and do whatever they think is best for me.

Now, I will show you how I would explain my plan to them.

I would treat it like a full-time job, if not more. I will wake up every morning at 5 am and start playing until 6:00 pm or 8:00 pm. I will do everything in that particular game. I will bump into every corner, find every bug, try my best to speed run and get noticed.

I would send that data to developers to improve my reputation. I would write the walk-through guides and post them on my websites. I would stream my video gaming and concentrate on followers. I would post recordings on YouTube and run ads on it.
I would interview game developers and other great game players via Skype to generate content for my followers. I would compete regionally and nationally playing video games. I would document everything that I do, every day. After three years, I would be making X amount of dollars from these

sources: YouTube ads, website ads, competition gaming, sales of walkthrough guides, guides on techniques, sponsors etc. After three years, I would publish my own book, *I Spent 3 Years Playing Video Games as a Business and I FAILED/ SUCCEEDED.*

If I succeed in making money out of this, the book would generate an additional stream of revenue for me so other people could buy and follow my examples. If I fail, the three years will not go to waste, as the parents of other kids will still be buying this book to showcase to their kids that this idea/business will not work for them. In other words, I will still be generating money from that.

I would bring only gamers to my Human Resources department. I would network with them at game conferences, I would DM (Direct Message) game developers and other super players like Ninja, who is making one million dollars per year playing games for sponsors. I would ask him to become a mentor and teach me.

I would spend my time for my Research and Development Department on YouTube and forums, reading up on how to improve my style of playing, as well as finding out when the next competitions take place.

IN THE REAL WORLD, THE SMARTEST PEOPLE ARE PEOPLE WHO MAKE MISTAKES AND LEARN.

IN SCHOOL, THE SMARTEST PEOPLE DO NoT MAKE MISTAKES.

-ROBERT KIYOSAKI

There would be no partying, no bars, no hangouts, and no movies. Every dollar and every minute would be used productively in my business.

I would spend my time developing my website and creating good thumbnails for my YouTube videos that attract and target my current audience already following me. I would learn and practice how to sell guides and techniques to my followers.

I would also learn how to pitch sponsors to support me or do shout outs to them on my YouTube or Instagram videos. Overall, I would treat it all seriously and not just as fun. At the end of the day, I promised my board of directors (my parents) that I will make money from it, and they will be waiting for weekly reports of my progress.

Do you recall that I have mentioned to you that failures are just as important as success stories? People love to read about the good and the bad. That's why the topics such as *10 Mistakes You Want to Avoid in Your Life* will be popular, just as much as *10 Things You Are Doing Right in Your Life.*

I am the CEO, and my success or failure will depend on the actions I take and how skillfully I spend the resources available to me. I know that there are hundreds of people who are dreaming to make this a reality.

SECTION 2. Summary of section 2

What would separate me from them? Ultimately, my love and my passion for video games will drive me forward to success.

THE ONLY REAL LUXURY IN LIFE IS TIME.

YOU'LL NEVER GET IT BACK.

SECTION 3.

AGGRESSIVE GROWTH

CHAPTER 13

PASSION DRIVER

I strongly believe that passion plays an important role in achieving success and results much faster than without it. Passion allows you to overcome your boundaries and leap into unknown territories without any fear. Funding your passion will give you an unfair competitive advantage over everyone else who is working 9-5 just for a simple paycheck. But how do you go about finding it? There are a couple of effective ways to go about it.

First, I would suggest paying attention to your time. When you enjoy doing something you will notice how time flies, whether you are watching a Game of Thrones episode, playing video games, exercising, or analyzing companies. If you just started doing something and in a blink of an eye 4 hours pass, then you are most likely passionate about what you are doing.

Another way to find your passion would be by simply trying multiple things. Go out with your friends, explore what they like to do. Pick up a part-time job in various fields. Read books and join various meetups and webinars. The point is to explore.

The mistake that the majority of people make is thinking they are passionate because of the money they are making. Let me tell you exactly what will happen. You might get into and organization selling Product X and make a lot of money.

You could get a new car, better house, and a bunch of other garbage to show off. Then you will need to constantly keep on working at that job simply to maintain everything you acquired.

Every day will become a horrifying Groundhog Day (great movie starring Bill Murray) repeat of the same thing, over and over. It will be the same cold calls every morning, the same lunch at the same exact time, and the very same nonstop quotas you have to meet every single day.

Trust me when I tell you that your passion will bring you money. It may not be a lot of money, but you will enjoy what you do every day. You will be able to leap into the unknown, experiment and try new things. You will accelerate your personal, professional, and financial growth over time. You will become an expert in the field you are passionate about. You will start publishing books, meet like-minded people, lecture and teach as much as you can. Your passion will help you gather and improve the right network faster. Your passion will drive you to correct, improve, and expand your skills. Your passion will help you to get you where you want to go and to be what you want to be.

Passion will always be the main driving force for your personal, professional, and financial growth. However, passion is not the only thing that can help boost your growth.

THE BIGGEST HURDLE IS REJECTION. ANY BUSINESS YOU START BE READY FOR IT. WHEN 10 DOORS ARE SLAMMED IN YOUR FACE, GO TO DOOR NUMBER 11 ENTHUSIASTICALLY, WITH A SMILE ON YOUR FACE.

-JOHN PAUL DEJOIRA

CHAPTER 14

TIME/MONEY MULTIPLIER

We have already discussed the importance of time and how valuable it can be. Most business owners try to recruit people and pay them X amount per hour. Business owners buy other peoples' time. After that, they convert that time into products or services and sell that for so much more, as we discussed in the beginning of this book. If you were hired by someone for $15 per hour and you don't produce enough business to at least cover your own payroll expenses, you become a liability and most likely will be fired. Now, as your own business owner, you can use time and/or money to speed up your own personal, professional, and financial growth.

Back in the day, in college, I paid a thousand dollars to learn this lesson. As I was a broke college student at the time, you can imagine just how painful it was for me. The time /money multiplier formula works like this: It simply multiplies what you actually desire. Let's take a look at a couple of examples.

If your desire is to multiply emotions, then the *time/money multiplier formula* (T/M MF) can help you do it. Imagine if I borrowed $5 from you, versus if I borrowed $50,000 from you. Suppose I am very late in returning the borrowed money to you. Because of this, your negative emotions will be equivalent to times 5 or times 50,000.

IF YOU PUT BANANAS AND MONEY IN FRONT OF MONKEYS, MONKEYS WILL CHOOSE BANANAS BECAUSE MONKEYS DO NOT KNOW THAT MONEY CAN BUY A LOT OF BANANAS.

IN REALITY, IF YOU OFFER A JOB AND BUSINESS TO PEOPLE, THEY WOULD CHOOSE JOB BECAUSE MOST PEOPLE DO NOT KNOW THAT BUSINESS CAN BRING MORE MONEY THAN WAGES' PROFIT IS BETTER THAN WAGES, FOR WAGES CAN MAKE YOU A LIVING BUT PROFITS CAN BRING YOU A FORTUNE.

Another example of how time/money multiplies emotions is: If I give you a pen for your birthday, versus I give you a Ferrari on your birthday, your positive emotions would be multiplied by the equivalent of the price tag of the gift. In some cases, a gift may be personally made or may not cost a lot of money, but it takes a lot of time to find it. In such a case, time would be the multiplier. So you see how T/M MF can easily multiply emotions.

It does not stop there. T/M MF can also multiply actions as well. If you pay $10 a month for a gym membership, and it's often raining or snowing outside, you may skip a day. On the other hand, if you pay $5,000 for a gym membership per month, you will most likely be sleeping there. You will never skip a single day. Again, your actions will be multiplied by the equivalent of time or money invested or lost.

Besides multiplying your actions and your emotions, T/M MF can also multiply your knowledge. For example, if a friend gave you this book for free. The amount of knowledge and information you will retain from this book would be equivalent to the time/money you spend on it. However, if by some miracle you paid $1,000 for this book, you would reread it multiple times and obviously retain more.

FINDING THE AMERICAN DREAM

Another example would be colleges, free online trainings, etc. When we go to college, we usually never actually pay for it.

You see, money for college is either borrowed as student loans and passed on to the institutions directly, or your parents pay for it. Because you didn't actually work for the loan money and didn't pay for it yourself, you most likely cut or skipped some classes. You probably didn't study as hard as you might have, and now you do not remember much of what you learned in every class. If you do remember something out of those classes, you most likely invested some of your other resources, which is time towards that particular subject. Let's be clear — in today's technological world, most anything can be learned online, free of charge. You can learn how to speak another language, play piano, make financial analysis, do your taxes, etc. Still, people end up investing their time and/or money for it, whether online or in person. Your chances of actually succeeding and accomplishing that goal is increased or multiplied by T/M MF.

As you see, because I paid $1,000 for that painful lesson almost fourteen years ago, I still remember it. Yet most of the college information I learned at the time has been, unfortunately, forgotten. Only the student debt is left to remind me that something was taught to me.

156   **SECTION 3.** Chapter 14. Time/Money multiplier

DON'T QUIT.

YOU'RE ALREADY IN PAIN.

YOU'RE ALREADY HURT.

GET A REWARD FROM IT.

Luckily for me, I use this formula to acquire new knowledge in various fields.

For instance, I have learned never to judge a book by its cover. You will meet a lot of people in your lifetime, and all of them have different backgrounds and various different experiences. Each of them may be more knowledgeable than you are in some area of life. That knowledge and experience may never be available to you again. So I love spending time meeting new people, just talking about their backgrounds, their challenges, and their ideologies or beliefs. I love taking new people I meet out for lunch, dinner, coffee, or just to hang out.

SUCCESS REQUIRES REPLACEMENT

REPLACE NETFLIX MARATHON WITH SLEEP.

REPLACE FAKE INFLUENCER WITH INSPIRING CREATORS.

REPLACE TOXIC FRIENDS WITH MENTORS.

REPLACE COMPLAINING WITH GRATITUDE.

REPLACE BLAME WITH RESPONSIBILITY.

REPLACE ALCOHOL WITH WATER.

REPLACE OVERTHINKING WITH ACTION.

I invest my time, which is super expensive, and/ or my money to pick up the bill as an investment to remember their stories and experiences, which helps me grow personally and professionally. I think it is a very small price to pay.

I use the same T/M MF in my businesses, as well. If I need to build a new sales structure for my company, I have two options to consider. First, I can spend one month learning how to create it, and then I could spend $4,000 and three months monitoring it. If it fails, I would use the data gathered from my first try and tweak it and spend another three months to see if it improves.

My second option would be to spend $10,000 to hire an experienced professional to establish the new sales model, a professional who has successfully created similar models for other companies. Spending $10,000 on the pro, I would ask questions and learn why this way to do something is better than not doing it.

I would still gather knowledge. I would have a proven model established without any failures, and I would save one month in researching and three months in monitoring.

My valuable time would be saved for other things.

In other words, I have bought a minimum of four months of my own time, established a new growth sales model, and acquired knowledge from the experienced professional for a mere $6,000 and not for $10,000, since I would have spent the first $4,000 or more to begin with on my first try out.

So how can you use the T/M MF correctly? If you have time and money, do not sit on it. Start investing in yourself. Start increasing your own value. Remember, your time is limited, and your money is just a tool. Don't acquire money just to sit on it and showcase how much you have. Don't spend time/money on stupid things. Invest. Invest in your knowledge. Invest in your business. Invest in your personal, professional and/or financial growth.

DON'T SLEEP LIKE YOU'RE RICH.

WORK LIKE YOU'RE BROKE.

CHAPTER 15

HAPPINESS UNLOCKED

As you begin uncovering things you are passionate about — things you want to do, things you absolutely love doing — you will begin investing with time and/or money. So first make sure as you are investing in X that it truly will make you happy.

Look, I know a lot of people who are making close to a million per year, and they are miserable. I also know people who are making 40K a year and are super happy. They got a job doing what they love. They are an asset to their company, and both they and the company know it. They live in Ohio, own a home, work from 9-5 without bringing problems home, spend their time with their wife and kids, and enjoy the barbeque on weekends.

As you move along with your life and business, surround yourself with like-minded people who do not judge you on what makes you happy. At the end of the day, it is your life. Do not be sucked into what society thinks you should be doing to be happy.

You may think owning a Ferrari will make you happy. Think again. How many hours will you spend driving it? And how many hours will you spend slaving at work to buy it, and how many more hours slaving to maintain it? And all of this — for what? Just so your friends will think you are successful, rich, and thus happy? Who cares what they think? The majority of the people you are currently surrounded by will likely leave your life. They will move to other states and go their separate ways. You will regret for the rest of your life if you let their judgments cloud your vision of what a happy life is for you and your family. Life is too short to be stuck doing things you don't really enjoy.

Now, I am not telling you to stop doing everything you're doing and abandon your responsibilities. I am saying you should be frank with yourself and concentrate your time and money on what you want to do and what makes you happy. This will allow you to remove all unnecessary burdens from your life. Your main goal should not be how much money you are making. It should be how happy you are.

BEHIND EVERY SUCCESSFUL PERSON, THERE ARE A LOT OF UNSUCCESSFUL YEARS.

YOU'RE NOT BEHIND IN LIFE. THERE'S NO TIMETABLE THAT WE ALL MUST FOLLOW. IT'S MADE UP. 7 BILLION PEOPLE CAN'T DO EVERYTHING IN THE SAME ORDER. WHAT'S EARLY? WHAT'S LATE? COMPARED TO WHO?

DON'T BEAT YOURSELF UP FOR WHERE YOU ARE.

IT'S YOUR SCHEDULE AND EVERYTHING IS RIGHT ON TIME.

CHAPTER 16

ACTION

Finally, you can read as many books as you want, attend as many lectures as you want, and visualize all your winnings. However, you will not get there if you do not act. Action and progression, no matter how small it is, will give you results. Whatever your goals are, without action they will stay only as dreams.

You have figured out what you are passionate about? What makes you happy? You have spent all your time and money buying online lessons and books, because you are worried you still are not there yet, that your skills in something else will simply embarrass you, and it will not be the best. It doesn't matter.

Everyone makes mistakes in the beginning. No one becomes a master overnight. In your first attempts, you will fail. You will look stupid, every now and then. Unlike others, the drones without any imagination, you are moving towards what you love. Remember you are passionate about that particular topic.

Be frank with others and yourself.

No need to showcase that you are a master.

You are not.

There is no need to lie to others or to yourself, either. Make mistakes along the way and learn from them. But under no circumstances stop. Continue and improve along the way, little by little.

If you follow everything in this book, you will be able to perform every day. It takes people years to learn, prepare, and become an overnight success. It took me six years, Monday through Sunday, with 18-hour days, nonstop, to get my business to where it is today. And I didn't even notice how fast it happened.

Of course, I made sacrifices along the way: I didn't see my newborn for two years straight. I have minimized all my expenses and leveraged all my personal time, including sleep, for 2 years, to graduate with a Bachelor of Science degree. Every minute of every day was put towards action to get me where I want to be, and I am not stopping here. There is still so much to learn and so much to try. There is still time to enjoy and love what I do. I know you can do the same.

IT'S NOT HOW EARLY YOU WAKE UP, OR HOW LATE YOU STAY UP, IT'S WHAT YOU'RE DOING WITH YOUR TIME WHEN YOU'RE UP.

-DAN SCHAWBEL

BE BRAVE ENOUGH TO SUCK AT SOMETHING NEW.

SECTION 3. Summary of section 3 + Conclusion

SUMMARY OF SECTION 3 + CONCLUSION

What is *your* American Dream?

If you are not living *your* American Dream, let me wrap up this book by challenging you. If you are willing to do the work, no matter where you are in life right now, you can claim the American Dream and make it your own.

I challenge you who believe that the American Dream is not possible for you. I ask that you dig deep, find your conviction, stand up, and reach for your dreams once more — this time with a new perspective and the ideas I shared with you in this book.

I challenge you to achieve *your own version* of the American Dream.

Remember, you already have everything you need to grow, and to grow much faster than you think. Pay attention to time so you can find your passion and your drive. Feel free to experiment and try new things. Invest in yourself by putting time and money to the best use through learning how to use the money multiplier formula. Understand that you are doing it for yourself.

It is *your life*, and no one should be telling you what you need to be happy. It is up to you. But most importantly, no matter what it is that you want or what you love to do, you need to start now — *right* now!

Now is the time. Send that email or DM, or make that phone call. Be honest and frank with yourself about yourself and about what you want to do and about what you want to become.

And, finally, **under no circumstances** sell out your happiness for a simple paycheck.

EUGENE GOLD

Eugene Gold is an entrepreneur, author, international speaker, and a mentor to many. When economy grows on an average of 11 % Gold's rare combination of strong business leadership, passion and experience has led him to the most exclusive clubs in business.

Showcasing a growth of more than 4400% in 3 years and earning top spots in the lists of INC 5000 in the years of 2018,2019 and 2020 as well as Entreprenuer360 in the years of 2016, 2018 and 2019.

His entrepreneurship, self-improvement and personal finance articles have been featured on websites such as Forbes.com, INC.com, Business.com and more.

Mr. Gold attended various events as a key note speaker to teach, mentor and inspire fellow entrepreneurs around the world. During this time, Mr. Gold has had the privilege of
sharing the stage with the likes of Les Brown, Kevin Harrington formerly of Shark Tank, Frank Shankwitz founder of Make a Wish Foundation, Sharon Lechter co-author of Rich dad poor dad, amongst many others.

Eugene Gold continues to be a committed philan-thropist by giving back to world communities such as Women of Global Change and Elite Meet as a benefactor and a volunteer and has been honored with numerous awards.